Moshi the Jackal

T. A. S. GIBSON

illustrated by the author

LONDON
REX COLLINGS
1977

Chapter One

The hot breeze stirred the grass as it moved over the African plains. Dustbowls covered the fauna of the savannahs with fine dust.

Sly paused in his territorial hunt and surveyed the parched landscape of the dry season. The breeze ruffled his golden fur and blew dust into his face. He closed his eyes and moistened his mouth.

His ears pricked up as he heard the shrill cries of distant hyenas, but he could not see them. He balanced himself on his hindlegs, scanned the seas of grass and whined as his sharp eyes picked out vultures wheeling in the sky and plummetting to the earth to feed. He watched the gathering of birds for a while, then moved towards them. Where vultures circled and dropped there was food.

Screeching, the scavengers moved in a chaotic chorus around him. Alerted, Sly moved on silently then stopped as he heard a rumble. The rumbling grew louder. Sly stood rooted to the spot as the sound vibrated through his body. He snarled and trembled. The roaring continued on all sides of him. Terrified, he turned his head to escape and was about to bolt when the roar ceased. He stood still. Everything was silent, then broken by a sharp scream.

A vulture, wild-eyed, its wings fanned out, burst through the grass and collided with Sly. The bird was the first to regain its balance. Beating its wings it became airborne stirring up the dust. Blinded, Sly clawed at the cloud of dust. Glimpsing the retreating bird's tail feathers the jackal snapped after them. There was a heavy crunch as the vulture ploughed back to earth and continued to retreat through the grass.

Sly dismissed the bird with a grunt and shaking the dust from his fur, he moved around to get his bearings. The hubbub of the scavengers had resumed but the hyenas' chattering had taken on a note of menace. This spurred him to move faster. He cleared a path through the mob of vultures.

A lion lay spread-eagled over a dead wildebeeste, its back to Sly, tearing mouthfulls of flesh out of the wildebeeste's flank and swallowing them whole. Between the lion and the hyenas lay a dead hyena which showed the success of the lion's surprise attack.

The hyenas had been panicked into flight by the lion's roar but now slowly drifted back to their kill. As their numbers increased so did their confidence. They manoeuvred around cautiously preparing to attack. The lion stopped eating and growled a warning.

Sly settled down to watch as three hyenas spurred on by the others, detached themselves from the pack and charged the lion head on. Sly slithered forward on his stomach.

The lion lifting itself on to its front paws, swung at the leader. A claw caught it in the throat and ripped out the jugular vein. Another blow caught the next hyena and sent it flying through the air with a broken back. The last hyena succeeded in penetrating the lion's defences, slashing a deep wound in the lion's shoulder before the lion clamped its jaws around the hyena's throat crushing it to death. Enraged by pain, the lion tensed himself to charge the pack.

As the lion launched himself at the pack, Sly saw his chance and leaped forward to sink his teeth into the shoulder of the dead wildebeeste.

He strained to rip a piece of meat from the carcass, but it would not give. Bracing himself he tugged again. Little by little, the meat came away. He jerked at it, trying to rip it away as out of the corner of his eye, he saw the lion bounding towards him. He scrambled backwards and cringed, feeling the wind from the lion's paw buffet him. He tried to dash away only to be knocked into the dust. He lay there, his eyes screwed shut, waiting for the death blow.

Nothing happened. Sly opened his eyes and saw, not the gaping jaws of the lion, but the beady eyes of a vulture as it pecked at the meat still firmly clamped between the jackal's teeth.

He looked for the lion and saw that it had turned to rebuff another hyena attack. The vulture continued to pull at the meat and was now joined by several others. Charging them, Sly tumbled down head first. Immediately he shot to his feet, still holding the lump of meat in his mouth and tried to charge, only to fall again as the weight of the meat proved too much for him.

A young hyena distracted from the fight with the lion by the jackal's awkward attempt to get food, threaded its way towards him through the vultures. Cackling, it came forward and grabbed a trailing piece of Sly's prize.

The two animals eyed each other, divided by the meat. Sly and the hyena pulled the meat in opposite directions. Outmatched in size and weight, Sly let himself be pulled, then sprang towards the hyena. He veered to one side. The hyena twisted its head awkwardly, allowing Sly to swing back to the other side.

The meat tore into two pieces sending the hyena and the jackal sprawling. Sly landed painfully on his tail while the hyena letting go of the meat, fell winded on its side.

Before the hyena regained his breath, Sly withdrew from the foray and ran until he had passed the termite mound, marking the inner boundary of his territory. Zig-zagging, he laid a false trail for any predators which might have picked up the dead wildebeeste's scent. Then he made for his present lair, sniffing cautiously as he went.

The lair was unusually quiet. He dropped the meat and flattened himself to the ground, calling softly towards the entrance. There was no response. He called again. A rustling came from within the lair. He wagged his tail to greet his mate. Apprehensively, he nuzzled

3

Silk. She was smaller than he and her fur was a lighter colour; below her belly four nipples hung heavy with milk.

She snatched the meat and blocked the entrance. Sly tried to squeeze past her but she growled. Yapping playfully he pranced with his front legs splayed out in front of him, his backside thrust into the air and wagging his tail. But Silk ignored him, concentrating on eating. He tried to get past her, but she nipped him on the nose. Sly looked puzzled at his mate who finished the meat and disappeared into the lair.

Sly followed her, crouching down at the entrance to poke his head into the darkness. Contented cries and gurgles reached his ears. Sly sniffed, then yapped at the sight of the four suckling cubs. He approached closer but Silk growled. Whining he laid his head down on his paws, and watched his first offspring.

*

The tall grass was freshly sprung since the fall of the first rains and had changed from a dry yellow to a lush green. The plains were dotted with large herds of game, crowded together and unaware of danger.

Taking advantage of the breeze stirring the grass, Sly and Silk moved towards a herd of Thomson's gazelles. They crept closer and closer, watching, sniffing, hidden by the grass.

The herd moved slowly under the watchful eye of the leader who, snorting and butting, sent any stragglers scurrying back to the herd.

Sly and Silk watched the buck's supervision, knowing that sooner or later he would have to break off to feed.

For some time the herd grazed undisturbed as the hunters awaited their opportunity to strike the untended young. A few does lagged behind lingering over young shoots, unaware of the imminent danger. The jackals waited expectantly, hoping that the leader would not return to reclaim the straying members of his herd.

Sly and Silk closed in on a doe and her fawn. They fanned out very quietly and inched nearer.

The doe grazed on. Each time she raised her head, the jackals disappeared out of sight. Soon they were ready to attack, but as Sly prepared to pounce his twitching tail rustled the grass. The doe, alerted, flicked her ears and thundered away.

Sly looked for Silk. She had gone as well. By the time he reached her, she had the fawn by the ear pulling it off balance.

5

Then the doe burst through the grass, charging with her horns pointed at Silk's belly. For a moment it seemed that the gazelle might hit Silk, but she released the fawn's ear and twisted out of harm's way. The doe gave chase as Sly moved in on the fawn.

The kicking fawn jabbed at Sly's neck with its sharp hooves. Sly did not notice that the renewed cries of the fawn had warned the doe of her offspring's plight. The mother rammed Sly on the rump. Stunned, he let out a yelp and released the fawn. The doe continued her attack putting Sly into full flight.

Then Silk took the unprotected fawn.

Sly looked behind him expecting to see the doe turn back to attend her distressed fawn, but she continued to pursue him. So intent was she on catching Sly that she did not hear the cries of her dying offspring.

Breathless, Sly tried unsuccessfully to shake off the doe until he spotted a haven. He sprinted for it, and plunged down the anteater's hole. The gazelle's hooves drummed on overhead.

Presently, Sly popped his head out of the hole; seeing that it was safe to return to Silk and her kill, he joined her and satisfied his hunger on the carcass. Then they made their way back to the lair to feed their hungry cubs on half-digested meat.

*

Since the beginning of the rainy season, Silk, now fully occupied with her four cubs, rarely joined Sly in the hunting. Sly was successful but the gazelles were gradually moving out of his territory as the grass grew too tall for them to crop. He sensed that this might be a sign of the wildebeeste's return from their annual migration, but each time he took up his vigil on the highest rock of his domain to survey their usual route, he saw no sign of them.

All too soon the small Thomson's gazelle had become so scarce that Sly depended on other sources of fresh meat.

The rains made hunting difficult. Frequently, Sly was forced by the torrential downpours to return to the den without food. Soon the cubs would emerge and Silk and Sly knew that if this present shortage of game continued, their young would starve.

If his day's hunting was unsuccessful, Sly would set out again in the wet darkness, leaving the sodden plains for the rocky outcrops to scour in the rain for grass rats, snakes, and insects. He scrambled over the slippery surface pawing and dislodging stones from under which small animals and insects scurried.

Each night he returned to the lair soaked and tired. He remained vigilant and slept near the entrance in case of flooding. There was nothing to do but sleep and hunt until the rain subsided.

The drumming continued but sounded louder. Opening his eyes, Sly listened. It was not rain. He moved up to the entrance. The rain had stopped but the drumming persisted. Wide awake, he worked his way out.

The ground steamed under the bright sun and Sly blinked his eyes in the sudden glare, saw what he wanted to see more than anything else.

The plains were black with snorting bodies, lowing and cropping the grass. The myriad grey shapes of wildebeeste streamed over the plains.

Something moved beside Sly, he turned. Silk had joined him. Soon the wildebeeste would be giving birth and then, finding food for the cubs would no longer be a problem.

Chapter Two

Looking out of the darkness of the den, Vivu, the boldest of the cubs stared in fascination at the droning insects collecting pollen. Attracted by the sound he crept out into the open, followed by Sheena and Fern. Their brother tried sniffing the insects but startled by their sudden whirr of wings under his nose shuffled back, bumping into his more cautious sisters.

Sly watched the first play of his three cubs. The last month had been hard foraging for food but the sight of the cubs moving freely outside the confines of the den now justified his efforts. He cuffed Vivu playfully and began to groom him, then Sheena and Fern.

As the fluffy cubs tottered away to look at things that were new to them, Sly moved towards the den to seek out the youngest of the litter. He slipped down into the dim interior of the den to find Moshi nuzzling sleepily against Silk.

Sly licked him but got no immediate response. Driven by her need to quench her thirst and hunger, Silk stretched and picked up Moshi in her teeth and went out into the sun. When Sly had joined her she left Moshi between his paws and headed across the plains.

He looked down at the helpless bundle and began to groom him. Moshi reacted by opening himself up then closing into an even tighter ball of fur. Sly placing a paw on Moshi's back legs unwound him ignoring his squeak of protest.

Blinking, Moshi lay adjusting himself to his new and open surroundings. At first all he could see was his father's paws and then the dusty blurr of his brother and sisters rolling on their backs. A groomed Moshi wobbled drunkenly to his feet and, keeping his distance from his romping brother and sisters, flopped down to continue his interrupted sleep, his mother's warmth replaced by the sun's.

Moshi's vulnerability excited Vivu. He saw his brother's furry underside as a target for pouncing practice. He crept up on the unsuspecting sleeper. Sheena and Fern abandoned their tussle and shadowed him. Forming a circle around Moshi they flattened themselves into crouching positions and prepared to pounce.

Sly watched his offspring's antics from his vantage point on top of the den then he looked carefully over the plains for approaching predators. Seeing nothing he settled down and dozed.

High above the circle of cubs, a vulture wheeled, its sharp eyes unblinking in the white sun. Its unfeathered neck, reddish-pink from the dried blood of a previous gorge, straightened out as it pin-pointed its sleeping target.

Yapping, the three little antagonists jumped and tugged at Moshi's body.

A dark shadow fell on the struggling brothers and sisters, startling the three attackers into scattering for the safety of the den.

Descending with a hiss of wings the vulture hooked its talons into the dazed Moshi.

Sly sprang. He hit the vulture with his body and tried to sink his teeth into the bird's neck. The vulture screeched under the unexpected weight of Sly and beat its wings in panic. Sly fell heavily to the ground. A wing smacked him on the side of the head. He reeled back.

Lips curled, he attacked again. The air filled with blinding dust and Sly's snapping jaws closed on nothing. He tried to see the vulture from within the dust but only saw an outline of the ascending bird with Moshi in its grip.

Sly leapt and sunk his teeth into the vulture's breast. The struggling bundle of fur and feathers hovered in the air, then crashed to the earth; tried once more for flight but fell back into the dust. The weight of the vulture crushed down on Sly. He fought to keep his hold but the pounding of the vulture's wings and weight was weakening his grip. In pain, he heard the wails of Moshi. He clamped harder with his teeth.

11

Suddenly the vulture released Moshi. His little body rolled away and slumped against a tuft of green.

The interlocked pair became airborne. The vulture, its talons free, struck at Sly's body,

12

leaving streaks of blood seeping through his fur. The combatants collided with a termite mound and slid down its side, the hard-packed earth rasping against the vulture's feathers. A shudder jolted Sly's body; he gasped and released his grip. The vulture shrieked loudly, beating its wings, trying to fly. Sly hurled himself at the neck and felt the bird's blood splatter his face. He bit deeper. The vulture sank down, flapping feebly in its death throes.

Sly closed his eyes and lay motionless over his kill. The dead vulture's talons were embedded in his stomach fur. Roused by flies, he knew that other scavengers would soon be attracted by the scent of blood. Sly tried to ease himself out of the grip of the corpse. Pained by his stomach wound he lay back. Then with a jerk he lifted himself free leaving clumps of his fur in the vulture's claws.

Ignoring his open wounds Sly stumbled through the grass in search of Moshi. He followed the trail of disturbed grass. He saw a small tuft of fur wedged between some grass roots and limped over to it.

Wounds lay across Moshi's body. The blood matted his fur and stained the grass a rusty brown. Sly licked and whined at the crumpled little form. He lifted Moshi, trying to avoid his wounds. Moshi stirred, but overcome by the pain he lost consciousness in his father's mouth.

Stopping to lick his wounds, Sly heard shuffling and sniffing behind him. Looking back he saw a trail of blood. He picked up Moshi and hurried on, keeping close to the ground to provide as much cover as possible. The scavengers had found the carcass. Sly could hear them tearing at the vulture and as his wound continued to bleed, he feared that the scavengers would soon be on his trail.

The hyenas stood looking mournfully at each other. All that remained of the vulture were the beak and claws. The leader sniffed at the scattered feathers and jerked his head up as he scented Sly's blood.

Silk was sitting on top of the den with the cubs. Even though she wanted to help her mate, she stood guard over her young. She had watched Sly and the vulture disappear from view by the termite mound. The cackles of the hyenas on the carcass had made her nervous but she stood her ground, frequently standing up on her hind legs looking for Sly's return.

The hyenas coming towards the den made her growl. The cubs drew nearer to her.

Leaping down she made to escape but stopped as she heard Sly's laboured breathing and frantic passage through the grass. She ran to Sly, took Moshi and darted off followed by Vivu, Sheena and Fern. She looked for Sly but he was not with them. Putting Moshi down she dashed back to the lair and nuzzled Sly trying to make him move, but he was too exhausted. She licked him for the last time and left him. The cubs had to be transferred to the safety of another lair.

Sly watched his mate retreat, too exhausted to follow. By the time he had recovered sufficient strength to move it was too late, the hyenas would be on him soon and he was now forced to act as decoy.

Moving to the den entrance he lowered himself inside, he licked his wounds. Rubbing his stomach on the packed earth, he stumbled to the suface. He heard the hyenas moving outside and, as he reached the cover of grass, the leader of the pack burst into the clearing in front of the den.

Warily, the hyena circled the dark opening but on seeing a bloody trail he began to dig the sides of the lair with the rest of the pack, convin'ced of an easy prey.

Sly watched them, and then limped away through the grass.

The leader edged down into the den, and finding nothing struggled back to the sunlight through the rest of the pack. Once more in the open, he traced Sly's hasty retreat into the grass.

Sly's stomach wound was still bleeding, slowing him down. His sight was blurred and the grass now looked taller. He shook his head but his vision would not clear. His lack of strength frightened him. He lost control of his front paws, stumbling.

The four hyenas followed their leader in silence. Occasionally he would sniff the breeze but kept on nosing forward, his head lowered to lick at the blood trail.

Exhausted, Sly got to his feet, turned back to face the way he had come and fell into the dust again. He did not see but listened. Whispers, scuffles, scurrying and then the rhythm of padding feet. He opened his eyes. The hyenas were near. His muscles tensed.

The hyenas movements began to vibrate down the grass. Sly tried to growl but could only croak. He looked above the grass just as the leader's ears appeared. Sly pushed down hard with his back legs. Around him the earth began to fall away. He tore at the grass to get a hold but was now suspended with his back legs swinging in the air. The hyenas were forgotten as he felt himself slipping frozen in a clawing position.

The hyenas' leader watched his prey vanish from view. He moved to the crumbling lip and saw Sly plunge into the swollen waters of the swift stream.

The cold water enveloped Sly's body as he sank beneath the surface and the bubbles trapped in his coat buoyed him up. The hyena watched his head disappear from view around a bend in the stream.

The growling leader tried to follow but found his way barred by thick thorny scrub. He yapped down at the water and wheeled away. The pack followed and the grass closed behind them as the flies fought over a drop of blood before the sun dried it.

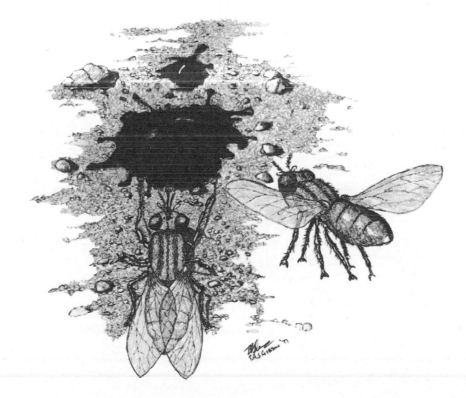

Chapter Three

Silk moved easily, her loping stride suited to the plains. She could hear the cubs panting to keep up, but she did not stop until their breathing began to be laboured and distant. She stopped and waited for them to catch up and, leaving Moshi with his brother and sisters to rest, she turned back and climbed a nearby termite mound.

Alert to signs of pursuing predators, Silk looked in the direction of the abandoned den. Nothing moved in the grass. She could see a few zebra but they gave no sign of being in danger so, reassured that she was not being trailed, she returned to her cubs. She repeated this lookout pattern whenever the cubs needed to rest.

So intent was Silk on watching for enemies that might attack from behind that she inadvertently cut a path through the grass to a dozing zebra. The yelping cubs scattered for cover. Silk dropped Moshi and bared her teeth at the surprised zebra, who backed away and bolted in fright. Still shaken, she sniffed the surrounding grass, but the strong scent of the zebra calmed her and calling the cubs she continued to one of their other dens.

Approaching the den, Silk hid the cubs. She stopped near the entrance to see whether it was occupied. She searched the thorn bush for fur scuffs and the opening for signs of disturbance. She entered the hole cautiously and, satisfied that the den was unoccupied, fetched her young and lay in the dark licking Moshi's wounds.

*

Sly thrashed the water with his paws to keep his head up. All around him there were rocks glistening in the swirling torrent. He tried to reach one but each time the water held him back. He tried to swim towards the bank but his body was pulled down by the undertow. Reaching up for the surface, he saw a red mist and pain forced him to open his mouth.

Bubbles streamed past his face and his body struck a rock then a roaring in his ears as the current pushed him to the surface. He clung to the rock, gasping for air. His body slipped on the rock as the current tugged at his back legs and tail. He tried to hold on, but fell back into the water and was swept on.

Sly felt the cold water numbing his body. He managed to keep his head up with his front legs splayed but his front paws were floundering out of the water. His body began to roll over. He tried to right himself but one of his paws caught on a branch of a dead tree straddling the stream. Pulling on the branch his head came clear of the water. As bark came away his claws sank into the wood underneath. The rotting wood forced him to shift his bleeding paws to a higher branch. Little by little, he raised his aching body out of the stream onto the dead tree.

Suddenly aware of the warmth of the afternoon sun, he edged his way, stiffly and sluggishly along the trunk to the dry bank, where he collapsed.

As his coat dried he recovered slowly and his first thoughts were of another lair nearby,

where Silk and the cubs had probably sought refuge. Even as he was already some way from it he scented them and knew he was right.

18

Moshi's wounds healed quickly and he was soon able to move out of the den and sit in the open. He was still weak and had to rely on his mother and father to regurgitate their kill for him.

Vivu, Sheena and Fern matured rapidly and were already eating from the kills and hunting insects and small rodents. Moshi, watching for his brother and sisters to return from their hunts, could hear them moving about in the grass. He wanted to be with them but he did not want to lose sight of the den's entrance which he could easily reach if sudden shadows came again. Whenever an unexpected movement startled him he scampered to the interior.

Vivu played upon his brother's fear of shadows; leaping over Moshi from the top of the den. At first a panic-stricken Moshi would make for the den tumbling, legs askew, into the entrance. However, it was not long before Moshi learned to hold his ground and Vivu looked elsewhere for play.

As Moshi's wounds healed beneath his fur, so did his memory of the winged attack fade. He now joined his brother and sisters in their play, and even though their games were rough, he always came back for more.

It was not long before the cubs were left on their own as increasingly Silk and Sly had to hunt together to find quarry to feed their growing offspring's appetites. Some times the cubs would go with Silk and Sly and watch their parents kill but generally in the afternoon the cubs would fall asleep in the grass. But not Moshi. He still did not feel at ease in the open and sought the shelter of a bush to sleep.

One afternoon as the cubs were dozing in the grass two glistening black eyes watched them from a flat triangular head out of which a forked tongue darted incessantly. The head lifted from the grass. When one of the cubs moved or twitched in its sleep, the head would freeze and silently slip from sight.

Flick, flick, the tongue began to move faster; behind its head the grass began to stir, revealing green-tinted coils glinting as ripples moved down its body.

The python appeared undecided, but gradually it moved towards sleeping Vivu. Coil by coil its body unwound, its head remaining motionless as its black eyes scrutinized the cubs.

The python's unwound trunk slithered across the dry ground to Vivu and silently began to encircle him.

Moshi stirred sleepily and looked around at his slumbering brother and sisters. The python stopped moving and stared at the waking cub. At first Moshi did not take in the snake but just as he was closing his drowsy eyes he saw the strange head of the python and sat up.

Moshi had never seen such a long, stretched-out creature before, suggesting stillness even when it moved, curving in and hugging the ground with its belly. He failed to see any harm in the motionless snake as he sat watching the elastic, shiny body continue to coil round Vivu. Moshi was tied to the python by its fixed stare until flies so irritated his eyes that he snapped at them and freed himself from the compelling black eyes. Suddenly Moshi saw the danger to his brother, uttering a warning yelp, but it was too late.

A thick coil whipped around Vivu's middle as he began to rise, then another curved in and

gripped him. Vivu cried out and crumpled under his weight.

Frightened and uncertain, Moshi rushed forward to the encircling snake and bit at one of the coils contracting around his brother's body. The python's head reared, straightened and struck at Moshi, butting him away.

Once more Moshi attacked the python's head not daring to look into the black eyes. The python evaded his assault with ease. Moshi persisted, ran forward, was pushed back, ran forward, but each time the snake curved away out of reach.

Vivu lay panting in the python's crushing coils. He could hear Moshi attacking but the weight of the snake made him helpless and all he could do was fight for breath within the folds of heavy flesh.

Tired, Moshi sat out of reach of the python which tightened its grip. Vivu gave a choking howl. Moshi sprung forward again growling, but the snake remained untouched by the young jackal's teeth.

At a safe distance Sheena and Fern sat and stared at the snake, yelping fearfully. Fixed to the spot they watched Moshi leap forward once again. But this time he fell exhausted in front of the python which lifted its expressionless head above him and with open jaws struck down at the limp cub, its long sharp fangs glistening with saliva. Moshi closed his eyes.

The descending head was torn from its wound-up body as Silk sprung to Moshi's defence.

Silk and Sly had returned just in time.

The coils loosened lifelessly and Vivu was free.

The cubs rushed to their parents for affection and reassurance. It was then that they realized they were hungry and that the dead python was food. Soon they were so gorged that they could do little more than lie and doze in the fading afternoon sunlight.

Moshi lay awake next to his sleeping father. He had proved that he was a useful member of his family. A swishing sound attracted his attention. Over his father's head he saw a vulture had landed on top of the den. As he trembled and whimpered, Sly awoke.

More vultures circled overhead and, as their numbers increased, the jackals tried in vain to drive them away. Realizing their lair was no longer safe Silk and Sly tore at their prey, and with their cubs retreated with mouthfuls of python.

21

Laden, the family moved off hurriedly with Moshi last in line. Still tired after his battle with the python and trailing his cumbersome piece of the carcass, he fell behind his brother and sisters. A vulture flew over him and he felt feathers brush him. The piece of python snagged in the undergrowth. The vulture made another pass and Moshi bolted.

The vulture became two vultures pursuing the fleeing cub. The meat they were after caught in a thorn bush. The vultures joined their shadows on the ground and closed in on Moshi with half-open wings.

Moshi tried to stand his ground but the familiar sight of these shadows, feathers and beaks overwhlemed his daring. He panicked and ran blindly through the bush which tore at his fur goading him on in his head-long flight.

Sly and Silk only noticed Moshi's absence when they stopped to rest at a safe distance from the den. They lay waiting for Moshi to appear but when they were ready to move on again and there was no sign of him, Sly set off in a search while the rest of the family made their way to the next den.

Moving slowly at first to try and pick up Moshi's scent Sly quickened his pace, casting from side to side and breaking off to climb termite mounds to scan the plains.

In the distance he saw two vultures pecking at remains in the grass. He charged down on them. The birds rose and circled away lazily.

When he saw the python's remains, he made a slight cry. He was now frantic. He picked up Moshi's scent and trailed it to a barrier of thorns. He called into the thicket, but there was no answer. He tried to enter it but the thorns kept him out. Giving up the search, he whined softly, threw back his head and howled.

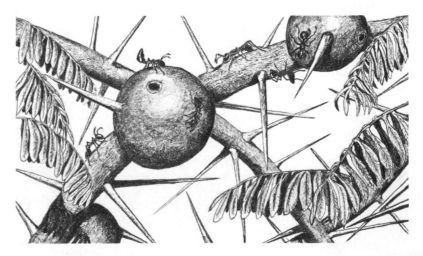

The rocky crags echoed his cry over the plains and, hearing it a long way off, Silk raised her head and took it up.

Chapter Four

Moshi awoke as the first rays of the sun filtered through the thicket. He blinked and moved his head out of the light. Pain jerked his head back until wide awake, he peered into the dark of the uncomfortable bush.

Tangled branches and thorny stems enclosed him on all sides. Looking for an escape he had a fleeting glimpse of grass through the thicket. He crawled towards it but the thorns held him back.

Moshi cried out to his absent parents for help. His wails not only went unheard but were overwhelmed by the continuous cries of waking birds.

A shadow fell over Moshi silencing his cries. He yapped hopefully. It moved away. He called out again. The branches moved in on him. He yelped as the confine of thorns pricked him. Weighed down, the stems cracked loudly and the branches were ripped away from the cringing cub, and he was enveloped by the pungent odour of a large animal.

The shortsighted, black rhino snorted and thrust its head through the foliage towards the strange sounds. The branches were a blurr. The great bulk pulled back and thrust its

horn deep into the bush, its thick hide indifferent to the thorns. The thicket's scent enticed the rhino to browse; it stripped thorns and leaves alike with its extended top lip and shovelled them into its mouth. Mucus ran from nose to lip preventing the thorns from piercing them.

The rhino munched on unaware of the cub, having forgotten the initial reason for its interest in the thorny acacia.

Saliva dribbled down and splattered Moshi. The stickiness and the smell made him screw his face up and back away. He crawled under some broken branches to escape the downpour from the rhino's mouth. Droplets still landed on his muzzle. Moshi snorted noisily.

The rhino gave an angry rumble and, lowering its head it tried to focus on Moshi. He shrank back. Hindered by its poor sight, the rhino backed away nervously, twisting its head from side to side and peering out for any sign of movement. Its horn caught on a branch, tearing the bush up by its roots and showering Moshi and the vicinity with earth.

The destruction ceased as abruptly as it had begun as the rhino convinced that it had vanquished its unseen foe, trotted away, tossing its tail.

Shaken but unhurt, Moshi crawled out from the uprooted branches and scampered away in the opposite direction.

The sudden temper of the dribbling, smelly animal had frightened and bewildered Moshi. He had yet to learn that a rhino was given to changeable moods, and that he could rely on his speed to escape the lumbering bulk.

The familiar surroundings of the grass calmed Moshi and soon he set about the difficult task of trying to satisfy his increasing hunger pangs and thirst. He sniffed close to the ground, disturbing ants and lice which he tried to lick up. But their smallness elluded his tongue. The dry soil aggravated his thirst. He nibbled the acacia leaves. At first, they tasted sweet, but as he chewed, the repugnant odour of the rhino filled his mouth. He retched and spat the leaves out. The taste remained. He dug at the roots of the grass and crunched the stems. The juices cleared his mouth but did nothing to quench his thirst.

The urge to reach water drove him to look for well-worn animal trails. He sensed that these might lead him to water. He sniffed the air and picked up the scent of wildebeeste. He followed the scent, stumbling on to a large track pitted with the imprints of many animals also searching for water.

At the sight of the pool he ran unheeding to the edge of the muddy water.

A head reared out of the mud. Startled, Moshi backed away as the gurgling mud sluggishly released the rest of the disturbed animal.

It stood looking at the cub with mud rolling off its body and head. Two yellow tusks thrust out on either side of its mouth as the old boar warthog lowered its head to charge.

Needing water, Moshi stood his ground. He flattened himself, the hackles on his neck up. He growled a warning.

The warthog remained motionless and silent. Its stillness deceived Moshi. He relaxed and moved nearer the water.

With an enraged squeal the boar charged the drinking jackal but the mud slowed down the boar and Moshi jumped clear of the tusks and escaped. The warthog did not give chase.

By the time Moshi had lapped his fill further down the bank, the boar was completely immersed again, only its tusks showing above the mud.

Moshi returned up the animal trail, having learnt to be cautious from the warthog and that persistence had quenched his thirst.

Moshi soon learnt to identify the sounds of his prey. Beetles, crickets, butterflies were watched, stalked and tasted. The inedible ones remembered.

Rasping wings attracted him. He pounced and bore the locust off. Dangling from his mouth by one of its rear legs, the insect wriggled and kicked out with the other leg, its spines sinking into Moshi's muzzle.

He yelped, and dropping the locust, looked at it with new respect. He put his paw on it. Both legs kicked again. The strength of the kick surprised him and he withdrew his paw quickly.

He moved to one side of the locust but it turned and presented him with rear legs again.

He tried to lean over the back legs and pick it up by the body, but it buzzed and flew straight up. Moshi ducked and then gave chase.

He was determined to catch the locust. Over the grass he bounced and as it landed he hit out with his paw. Knocked off balance the locust fell on its back, and Moshi placed his paw quickly on the soft underbelly and nipped off the locust's back legs.

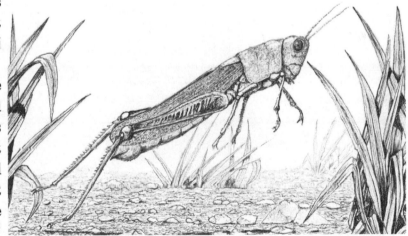

Having mastered the locust he chewed berries and fruit which had ripened during the rains and lay rotting on the ground.

Bloated, he found shelter in the upturned roots of a tree to sleep. As the sun set, the sleeping cub curled himself into a smaller ball and pulled closer to the wood for warmth, but the hard bark was no substitute for Silk's fur.

He shivered as the early morning mist covered him with dew. He opened his eyes and shook himself, still tired.

At night, the plains took on a new menace. While he tried to sleep, zebra and wildebeeste had browsed so close to him that he had felt the vibrations of the grass being cropped as the grazers moved by. In the dark, the unknown hunting calls kept him alert, and he had lain ready to bolt at the slightest sign of discovery.

The sun dispersed the mist. Moshi stretched and warmed himself. He went back to scavenging for berries. He chewed them, listening to the sounds of the insects which his stomach depended on to be full. Busy scratching attracted his attention.

He stopped eating and pricked up his ears to locate the scratching. It was close, but nothing moved until Moshi saw the droppings of a large animal. He watched without going towards it.

The old dung was broken into balls. One of them rocked. He stared at it, his head on one side, as the ball rolled ponderously towards him. Moshi backed away. Reaching an incline the ball gained momentum leaving behind an enormous black beetle, the biggest Moshi had ever seen. He watched the industrious beetle plod laboriously after the ball. It turned around, lifted its back legs, and began to push again.

Moshi teased the beetle by pushing the dungball away. Seemingly oblivious of the jackal's interference, it followed its ball, propelling it along slowly.

Still hungry, Moshi decided to sample this helpless insect. He flicked it on its back and watched the beetle's legs wave helplessly in the air, and then bent to snap it up. A leg

caught his muzzle and in an instant, the beetle had righted itself and clamped securely on the top of Moshi's nose.

The beetle's clawed feet pricked Moshi's sensitive muzzle. He shook his head violently and panicked as he felt the insect's grip tighten. His eyes watered, blurring his view of the beetle. Moshi brushed at it with his front paws but they slid over the smooth shell which protected the beetle's back. He tried to run away from the clinger, forwards, backwards, stumbling and falling through the grass.

The beetle remained on Moshi's nose. Exhausted, Moshi stood still and squinted at the immovable insect waving its antennae. Then it slackened its grip slightly. Moshi lifted his paw to brush it away but thought better of it. Wings spread from beneath the shell and the beetle flew off in silence. Moshi watched it dip down to the ground and then with a loud drone fly up and drop back in a silent glide to the safety of the grass.

Moshi brushed his muzzle and once more set about hunting for insects, but not dung beetles.

Sniffing around, a distant jackal call sent a shudder of excitement through him. He followed the call, picked up the scent of the jackal, and let out a cry of delight. The scent was not family, but at least it was of his own kind.

A lean body charged Moshi. He was picked up by the ruff of his neck and flung into the air. The cub lay winded. A paw was placed on his chest and the silver-backed jackal curled back its lip and growled.

Moshi's whimper was an appeal which provoked the jackal to bear its teeth more aggressively. Terrified, Moshi lay silent.

The jackal lifted his paw slowly and sniffed the young jackal all over. Moshi tried to cover his rear with his tail but a growl made him stop.

When the silver-backed jackal had finished his inspection of the golden cub, he growled again and loped away. Moshi cried out after the retreating jackal and followed him in a crouched, submissive manner. The lone jackal snarled at him to stop. He ignored the warning. He did not want to be left on his own. The jackal leaped at Moshi biting his head and legs. The yelping cub cowered down.

The jackal left Moshi and continued on his way. Moshi watched the withdrawal and cried out again to be allowed to follow, but the jackal ignored his plea.

Moshi continued to watch and call out for a long time after the jackal had vanished from view. Eventually he limped off, his yearning for his own kind undiminished. It led him deeper into the plains, tracking and following any signs of his own kind, stopping to hunt only when a trail or scent became too difficult to follow.

Chapter Five

Moshi's quest led him on an erratic course over the plains, bringing him into contact with many animals, most of which showed little interest in him.

He learnt to ignore animals which were neither a direct threat to his life nor a source of food.

At first, elephants frightened him, but the insects that they disturbed during their browsing soon had him following in their wake.

This was easy hunting and as the elephants ignored him, Moshi took to following herds without fear, but not for long.

Following a browsing herd, Moshi was so engrossed in chasing a locust that he failed to see that an elephant had fallen behind the herd to scratch itself on a termite-mound. Each time he got near enough to catch the locust, it flew a few more feet up the trail. Watching where the elusive insect landed, he stalked it again. He crept nearer, and as he sprang, the locust moved again. Moshi's head slammed into a rear leg of the elephant.

Trumpetting, the elephant charged for the herd while a stunned Moshi stumbled to his feet to be confronted by a wall of tusks and trunks. He stopped in his tracks, then terrified, he bolted.

As the weeks and months passed, Moshi's reliance on the insect world for food lessened as he grew more adept in hunting rodents, particularly the grass rat.

When he first attempted to hunt these little rodents they eluded him easily. Their scurrying through the grass as he passed would draw him to the chase, but fruitlessly. Following one rat's retreat, his clumsy pursuit sent other rats darting in all directions, provoking him to give chase until he was running round and round in circles.

However, in time, he learned to approach the rats noisily, and then sitting quietly, he heard the rats return to feeding. He listened to the rat nearest him and watched the top of the grass for the slight vibration of the stems which showed the rat's exact position. Then he sprang forward to catch his food.

The struggle to survive without the protection of his family toughened him. He lost his

fluffy cub coat and took on the thick longer fur of an adult. And though still not full grown, his body became lean and wiry as he wandered ever on.

Moshi's attempts to join other jackals did not succeed. Small scars around his ears and face told of many painful meetings with his own kind while crossing their territories. A fresh scab on his shoulder had been inflicted by a jackal who had tolerated Moshi around his mate until the immature jackal sought maternal affection which was mistaken as courtship.

To avoid further wounds, Moshi took to travelling at night. Twilight suited him.

The calls of jackals as they followed the hunting hyenas and lions made him howl and scamper to the foray where he remained a spectator, neither hunter nor prey. At dawn Moshi would often venture down to the remains of a kill and pick around the carcass before the vultures arrived.

At the first sign of the aerial scavengers he would leave off eating and seek out a place to

sleep through the heat of the day. In the cool of early evening, Moshi awoke, hunted for rodents, and then made for the waterhole.

It was on one of these forays, approaching water that the commanding roar of an attacking lion shattered the evening stillness.

Moshi stood listening to the terrified cries of a dying zebra. Cautiously, he moved towards the sounds. Emerging from the grass, he saw a lioness dragging a zebra in its death throes from the waterhole to her waiting mate. When the lions had pulled the carcass into the bush, he darted to the waterhole, lapped hurriedly, and then followed the lions.

Finding cover in the shadows of a bush, Moshi watched the lions feeding and smelt the alluring scent of warm blood. He waited for them to eat their fill and move away. This was the first time Moshi had reached a kill before other scavengers.

The lions having finished, did not move away, but lay resting on their full stomachs. Moshi became restless, and then, alarmed as he noticed signs of other scavengers slinking through the bush. As he moved in closer, the sight of another jackal edging round to his hiding place made him retreat and put his hackles up.

Moshi growled a warning and the other jackal peered into the shadows. He growled again and then of a sudden sat in silence watching his own father staring at him in the darkness.

Moshi chirruped and hurried up to Sly, nipping him with affection around his muzzle.

Sly snarled at the half-grown jackal, now prone in a submissive position. He sniffed, then sniffed again, and suddenly recognizing Moshi's scent, wagged his tail in greeting.

A warning rumble from the sated lioness made both jackals break off their reunion and scatter. Only when they realized that there was no pursuit did they come together again.

Now, expectant scavengers filled the bush. Hyenas moved about impatiently while the trees around the carcass were laden down with vultures fighting for a perch.

Beside Sly, Moshi felt secure and unafraid. Once father and son had a vantage point near the half-eaten zebra, they lay down and watched the lions and hyenas confront each other.

The lion and lioness lay with their eyes closed. Only their twitching tails showed that they were not sleeping.

Then a hyena broke cover and sneaked towards the zebra. It paused, eyes fixed on the lions.

Moshi heard Sly growl softly.

The hyena crept closer, followed by another.

Both lions' tails were still but as the first hyena reached the carcass, the lions attacked, silently and swiftly. The first hyena died quickly as the lion caught it by the throat, ripping its head from its body. The second hyena shrieked in terror, scrambling clear of the charging lioness.

Spurred on by their success, both lion and lioness pursued the hyena.

Before Sly and Moshi were able to get to the unguarded carcass, other hyenas moved in, chewing at the zebra in a tight pack.

Sly and Moshi slunk back to wait their turn.

Two angry roars heralded the lions return who immediately attacked the feeding hyenas.

The cries of dying hyenas filled the air. Panic broke out as the jackals and remaining hyenas fled as one. A black cloud of vultures lifted from the trees as the lions gave chase to the scattering scavengers.

Sly and Moshi ran side by side and only slowed to a trot beyond the bush.

*

Moshi's welcome by the rest of the family was mixed. Sheena and Fern showed their affection by playing with him and grooming him, but Silk held herself aloof and rebuffed his attempts at affection. Moshi persisted and his mother allowed him to groom her but, it was only after he had been with the family for some weeks that she showed her affection by grooming him.

His brother Vivu tried to dominate him but resisting, Moshi snarled and bit Vivu about his muzzle and throat. Both brothers reared up on their hindlegs, snapping and growling, until Sly charged between them. They separated to form an uneasy truce.

The cubs could now fend for themselves and took to exploring and hunting on their own while remaining at the lair and sharing in whatever Silk and Sly brought back. Sheena and Fern kept close to the lair but Moshi and Vivu scoured over the whole of Sly's territory, and spent days away, returning to the family meeting point, at different times from each other, whenever possible.

This routine continued until Silk became heavy with cubs and was unable to hunt for herself.

Following the birth of the cubs, Sheena and Fern stayed with Silk tending the new offspring, and though Moshi and Vivu still hunted apart, they were forced to join together with Sly to hunt for gazelle.

The three hunters were so successful that there were soon many caches of birds and rodents buried around the lair. When they set out to hunt the gazelle, the brothers relied on Sly's greater knowledge of his hunting grounds to find the gazelle fawns.

When Sly singled out a fawn for attack, Moshi and Vivu waited for the doe to attempt a rescue which they foiled by nipping at her flanks, harassing her until the fawn's cries had been silenced by death.

Early one evening as Moshi and Vivu regained their breath after drawing a doe away successfully, they heard Sly bark in alarm. Growling and bristling they loped to his side. He stood by the dead fawn. Moshi whined and licked his father, but he growled louder and stared at the grass behind the fawn. He backed away and growled at Vivu and Moshi to follow but his sons stood and watched him.

Suddenly, a leopard sprang up out of the grass and stood over the fawn. Its slit-eyes gleaming as it drew back its mouth in a snarl.

Sly continued to retreat, but Moshi and Vivu stood their ground and returned the leopard's snarl. The brothers split up and circled the cat in opposite directions, to harrass it as they had done so often with gazelles.

Sly barked a warning but it was too late as Vivu and then Moshi sprang forward. The leopard hissed and swung round to face Vivu. Swiftly, Moshi leaped to the attack and sank his teeth into the leopard's tail and withdrew.

The cat roared in pain and twisted round.

Vivu charged forward. The leopard faced him again as he leaped over the cat, unclawed.

The young jackals having lost their advantage were in front of the leopard, too close to be able to circle back again without opening themselves to attack. Moshi and Vivu growled and tried to bait the leopard to give chase but it ignored them, lay down on its side and licked itself.

Sly even more alarmed, called out continuously but his offspring were concentrating on the chance that the cat had given them to attack its vulnerable underside.

Unable to resist the temptation, Moshi dived towards the leopard's stomach. At the same time, Sly shot past Vivu, veered in front of Moshi and pushed him to one side.

The leopard lashed out with its front paws and caught Sly around the neck before he could spring clear. It sank its jaws into Sly's throat and clawed at Sly's body with its back legs. The cat tossed the dead jackal aside with a final kick and sprang up alert for another attack from the other jackals.

Moshi and Vivu turned tail and fled.

The leopard bounded after them then stopped. It grunted and without a second glance at the dead jackal, sucked the warm blood of the fawn.

Chapter Six

In the wake of her mate's death, Silk became listless and disinterested in the new litter. She ignored the cubs mewing for her milk, lying on her own outside the den and eating listlessly.

Sheena and Fern tried to entice her near her cubs but she lay down and did not respond until Sheena brought one of the cubs to her.

Silk snarled and snapped at it.

Moshi and Vivu hunted separately again. Permanent rivals, the demand for food was the only thing that stopped them from fighting for the position of dominant male.

At last, Fern succeeded in getting Silk to take some interest in her cubs, but not before two of the litter had died. Fern had picked up one of the starved cubs and ignoring Silk's growls dropped it in front of her and left her.

Silk ignored the dead cub for a while then sniffed it and then a little later, licked it, and coaxed it to suck. The lifeless cub rolled limply in her paws.

By the time Fern brought the second cub, Silk was on her feet, and seeing it dead, returned to the lair.

Despite little milk, the two remaining cubs lived as Sheena and Fern fed their mother half-chewed prey. Within six weeks they had been weaned, and Silk was able to leave them in the care of their half-sisters, and hunt.

Tension increased between Vivu and Moshi as they vied for the dominance of Sly's territory. Each in turn tried to gain Silk's favour but without success. They would have mated her but when they came too close, she growled and bit them on the muzzle.

After repeated rebuffs Moshi gave up and took to staying away on his own. He noticed that a change had occurred on the plains. The wildebeeste and zebra were gathering into large herds. He had to be careful in some places to avoid being trampled on. Usually timid, the massing animals became bold and erratic, sometimes chasing animals that came too close to them.

Lions, cheetahs, packs of wild dogs and hyenas were attracted by these massing herds. A hunt by these predators created havoc, especially the pack animals who because of the close numbers of their prey killed more than they ate. Even so, the growing herds felt no losses. The rumble of their tramping and bellowing filled the plains. A thunder which went on unbroken, day and night. Even the roar of a lion on a kill went unheard.

Watching these increasing herds, Moshi met many more of his own kind. With so much food to scavenge there was no fighting among themselves for the territorial jackals tolerated strangers.

Even the vultures, overeating, became too lazy to squabble. If one carcass was overcrowded, they simply lumbered into the air and flopped down onto another.

Many predators also died, mostly the young. Hundreds of thousands of wildebeeste were not only threatened but were a threat in themselves. A young predator on its first kill could find a moving wall of wildebeeste being forced towards it by its own pressing numbers. If an inexperienced predator lunged to defend its prey, it would be trampled and gored to death.

Sometimes the wildebeeste spotted a lion or cheetah before it could spring a surprise attack. The hunter was forced to flee the hunted.

When Moshi saw a cheetah fleeing for its life, pursued by twenty wildebeeste he learned to be on constant alert. When eating from a wildebeeste, he kept a cautious eye on any wildebeeste grazing nearby.

Soon the herds were a million or more and ready for their long, timeless trek. Their movement forward was not apparent until the plains began to clear, leaving behind a web pattern of paths becoming the deep trenches made by the millions of hooves as they fell into line and marched, one behind the other.

Within a week, the plains were quiet. The thunder had passed. The dry season commenced as the few stragglers followed the vast, trailing columns of dusty migration.

During the massing, Moshi had returned only twice. Each time to signs that the family was breaking up. Sheena had drifted away and paired with a jackal from a neighbouring territory, and though he had seen her mate and her around the herds, he did not approach

41

her. Fern remained at the cave and took care of the cubs who were already becoming independent. Silk and Vivu were absent during Moshi's two visits. He waited restlessly for Silk to appear then returned to the plains.

Now that the herds had departed, Moshi returned once more to the lair. An outsider, another jackal had joined the family. Fern and the cubs greeted him but Moshi growled when he saw Vivu lying next to Silk, grooming her.

Moshi barked out a challenge to his brother's dominance and charged Vivu. Taken off guard, Vivu launched himself straight at Moshi who swerved to one side and bit into his brother's shoulder, drawing first blood. Snarling, Vivu swung round and snapped at Moshi's ear, then reared onto his hind legs to bite Moshi on the back of his neck. Moshi leapt up, and both jackals stood on their hindlegs biting each other about the face and neck.

Vivu using his extra weight, forced Moshi to lose his balance. Moshi fell. But before Vivu could bite him across the throat, he twisted and took the bite on the protective ruff of the back of his neck. Moshi was pinned; blood trickled down his neck as Vivu sunk his fangs deeper to make Moshi submit. But Moshi did not submit. He growled and fought on, twisting and squirming under Vivu's weight. Ignoring the pain, he brought his legs under himself, and with all his strength leapt into the air.

Vivu let go. Thrown by his sudden loss of advantage he tried to topple Moshi over, but Moshi was ready for him, recoiling away, instead of resisting. Caught off balance, Vivu fell heavily, letting out a winded grunt. He landed on his side rolling onto his back exposing his throat.

Moshi sprang forward to sink his teeth in, but before he could, Silk flew at him. She sent Moshi sprawling in the dust. When he stood up, Silk, Fern and Vivu faced him as one, snarling. He snapped back weakly. They nipped and bit him around his flank, forcing him to run. Chasing him to the edge of Sly's territory, they left him beaten.

Moshi knew he would never join his family again. He was an outcast.

*

Moshi felt his banishment as the dry season left its mark. He poached and scavenged over

42

the other jackal's hunting ground without much trouble, but as the heat burnt the earth, and dried up the waterholes, the game became scarce.

The jackals with territory, banded together in packs and then split into groups of three or four and jealously guarded their boundaries. Together they hunted Thomson's gazelle successfully, and prevented any marauding lone jackals from scavenging around kills made by other predators.

Moshi found himself harassed as the packs forced him to dodge from one territory to another. To avoid starvation, Moshi hunted throughout his waking hours, even in the hottest part of the day when most animals rested. His hunting forays yielded little as most of the smaller plains animals he now relied on, were underground, escaping from the heat. Occasionally, as he padded quietly through the grass he flushed a Franklin bird, but mostly he dug and grubbed for insects.

The sun became unbearable as he sniffed and scratched around in the dust. He gave up and stood aimlessly watching the haze distort the distant termite mounds. Today, even insects were difficult to find.

He shook himself and forced his tired eyes to pick out a place to rest up. A small bush growing out of the base of a termite mound caught his attention. He ambled towards it. Nothing stirred or made a sound as he passed. The plains were deserted.

Moshi lay down in the thin shade of the bush. His rest would not last long because at the first sign of the heat dropping, the jackal packs would be on the move, and Moshi would need all his strength and guile to survive another day. Panting, he stretched out on his side and dozed.

A very faint rasping on the dry earth of the termite mound, woke him instantly. He raised his head and stared. Somewhere up in the crevasses a snake was resting. He stood up and sniffed and scratched at cracks and holes.

Moshi knew only one way to catch this elusive prey; to force it to strike at him. A hiss made him jump back. The snake was in a rat hole behind the roots of the bush. He must get it out into the open. Hunger urged him to dig faster. The earth crumbled and fell away easily. Alerted for any sign of the snake, he heard its coils unwinding, and jumped back as it emerged from the hole.

Moshi watched as the snake reared up and a hood spread around its head. One bite from this cobra would kill him. Moshi edged around it, until he stood between the snake, and the rat hole. The slight fall of earth as his tail brushed the mound made him snarl. The rat hole covered, Moshi yapped and lunged at the cobra. In an effort to make it escape through the grass where he could bite along its outstretched body before the cobra could strike back. But the cobra remained reared up in front of him and only arched its head back at each attempt to make it slide away.

Moshi growled uneasily at the cobra's stillness. The snake's tongue flicked in and out and Moshi tensed as he watched it weave from side to side and glide towards him. As the snake attacked, Moshi retreated, forgetting that he was up against the mound. Earth crumbled between his legs. He jumped. The cobra struck.

Moshi saw the sunlight glint on its scales as it lunged and twisted in the air. The fangs barely missed his shoulder and he felt the cobra's hood brush by his coat. He turned his head and snapped at the extended body, biting it halfway down its body. He let go and leaped back in time to avoid the turning snake's strike at his neck. Shaken, he hesitated, watching the hissing cobra curl its long body into a protective loop. Then he noticed that beneath where he had bitten, the cobra was having difficulty in curling its body. Quickly he darted forward, forcing the cobra to strike to protect its exposed tail. Repeatedly, he harassed the snake, watching it sink lower and lower, until it hardly lifted its exhausted head. Moshi leaped and crunched through the back bone below its hood.

Moshi could only eat half his kill before he was full. It had been the largest snake he had hunted on his own. He dozed under the bush until the first rustle of the smaller animals emerging from their burrows to feed, warned him that it was time to move on. Warily he returned to feed on what was left of the cobra but was immediately disturbed by the sudden clap of a frightened bird, as it flew up out of the grass in the distance.

He scrambled up the termite mound to get a better view over the plains. A faint breeze stirred his back as he tried to see what alarmed the bird.

The few remaining zebra and wildebeeste browsed unconcerned but some Thomson's gazelle nearest him were bunched together and were too agitated to graze. He strained forward to catch a glimpse of what they were all staring at.

He raised his hackles and growled, softly. Four jackals were moving one behind the other, loping along, showing little interest in the watching gazelle.

Moshi relaxed as they continued on without turning in his direction. They vanished into the grass again, but caution prompted him to keep watching. He sat half-way down the mound waiting for them to break cover again.

The jackals were nearer but still heading in a direction away from the mound. The leading jackal paused and sniffed into the breeze. Before it turned, Moshi knew that he had been discovered and was sliding down the loose surface of the mound on his haunches.

Growling, he stood up and shook himself free of the billowing dust. He snarled in reply to the yaps of the approaching jackals whose leader had spotted the dust rising over the top of the termite mound.

Moshi raced for their territorial boundary. As he ran he looked back, but the jackals were nowhere in sight. He loped on, but hearing no cries of pursuit, he stopped and stood up on his hindlegs to look back at the mound.

The jackals were by the small bush eating the remains of the cobra.

Moshi raced under cover of the grass circling and zig-zagging back and forth over his trail, then he sped towards higher ground.

The jackals followed again.

46

Moshi crawled to the top of the rise on his stomach and watched the jackals below. His pursuers had scattered and were trying to trace his scent which was soon covered by their own scents.

Moshi slipped down the other side of the rise and openly trotted away. He saw the familiar pattern of migratory paths criss-cross through the sparse grass carving their way towards the first slopes of the blue hills in the distance. He became excited as he sniffed the faint scents of the wildebeeste and zebra.

In the hoof-trenches, the smell was so strong he could almost taste the meat. He followed the trail, then stopped torn between the urge to stay close by his own home grounds or to follow the scents. He went on a bit further, sniffed again and continued up the slope.

Moshi heard the distant howl of a jackal echo up from the vast yellow plains below. He whined in reply but continued on.

The spell of the savannahs was broken.

Chapter Seven

As Moshi climbed higher along the trail the grass slopes gave way to acacia trees and thorny thickets. In the waning sunlight, the umbrella-shaped foliage of the acacia cast deep flickering shadows on the stony ground.

Moshi stopped and sniffed. Over the scents of the migrants he caught the smell of leopard. Frightened that the danger might still lurk in the shadows, he retreated to the grass and curled up to sleep. When the shrill cry of a tree hyrax shattered the peace, already unnerved by the leopard smell, Moshi shot to his feet and stared wildly around as another scream followed. Shaking, he retreated further back.

All night the strange and hostile cries of the nocturnal creatures in the scrub kept him awake and a welcome silence only fell when the dawn broke.

When Moshi awoke, he ventured back to the thickets. The light from the rising sun had broken through the shadows and he could see clearly along the migration paths. Warily, he moved down them, searching for traces of the conflict he had heard throughout the night. But there were none and instead he found an abundance of rats and mice. Hungry, he hunted.

The deeper Moshi penetrated the thickets the less distinct the paths became as the migration had split and the animals had invididually worked their way through.

Moshi tracked by the sight and smell of the hair combed from the animals as they had brushed against the thorns and branches. Often he was misled by the smell of dead animals which had been too weak or too old to disentangle themselves once they were trapped but gradually the bush thinned and he found where the herds had regrouped.

The trail wound its way over hot plateaus and thick forests, then meandered back to the acacia scrub. Moshi tracked by day and rested through the night. His easy loping stride covering the miles quickly, until he reached the grassy regions of the highland plains. There he saw the first signs of the migration slowing.

Soon, he encountered small herds of stragglers browsing and as he ran past them he could feel the vibration of the main body under foot.

Veering towards higher ground he rested and watched, slowly absorbing the pattern of life below.

Waves of animals were breaking out of the column and fanning out to graze. Though they all moved in the same direction, the urgency and pace they had maintained since leaving the savannah was gone as they paused to crop hungrily at the grass.

A lioness's attacking roar echoed out, sending a shudder of excitement through Moshi. He watched the grazers scatter as she lunged at a zebra and landed on its back. Squealing, it crumpled under her weight, dying with its neck breaking from the impact.

Panting, the lioness stood over the carcass and then started to drag it to her waiting cubs while the grazers returned to watch.

Moshi waited until the first vulture was circling above to guide him, then he moved down amongst the herds. When he reached the lioness she was chewing noisily on the zebra's intestines while her two cubs tried to bite through the tougher and less tasty part along the zebra's back.

He moved closer to the cubs in the hope of stealing some scraps, but the lioness stopped eating and watched him. He slunk back.

Two other golden jackals approached. Growling Moshi sank down into the grass and crept towards them. The pair were so intent on watching the feeding lions that Moshi's

attack caught them by surprise as he charged straight into the leading jackal and knocked it to the ground.

Snarling, he stood over it, his fangs inches from its throat. The jackal whimpered but he ignored it and continued to growl until its companion had quailed before his gaze.

Lying down, it crawled towards him on its stomach, he growled louder and made as if to attack it. The submissive jackal lifted its front paw brushing its muzzle. Moshi stopped and backed away.

Curling his lips back, he let them approach and sniff, then assured of his dominance he wagged his tail.

Eagerly, the two accepted the token of friendship and licked his face. He tolerated their affection until they tried to entice him to play. Growling at them to stop he turned back to the lions. As they did not follow Moshi stopped and wagged his tail. They scampered to him

and the three of them pushed their way through the vultures to the kill.

The lioness and cubs had continued to feed, undisturbed by the jackals. With the abundance of game, the lioness, like other predators, was resigned to the gathering scavengers in the same way as they were forced to accept the swarms of flies that congregated around them after every kill.

Occasionally, the lioness had glanced at the scavengers but only to see if any hyenas had joined them.

The two.other jackals shadowed Moshi as he crept up to the kill and lay down to wait. It was not long before the lioness finally stretched and, licking at the blood smeared around her cubs' faces, lazily walked away with the youngsters waddling behind, their stomachs swollen from over-eating.

The three jackals pounced as one, tearing at the remains and between bites snapped at the overeager vultures.

Moshi gulped down the flesh hungrily, but the persistent rustle of a bird closing in made him turn. He snapped, then his hackles rose at the sight of two silver-backed jackals behind the vulture.

His mind flashed back to his cubhood encounter and, barking a warning, he ran at them.

Only seeing one golden jackal the two silver-backed charged; the distinctive black and silver speckled fur along their backs bristling. Just as they reached Moshi, two golden balls of fur leapt on them from either side.

Trapped and outnumbered, the silver-backs fought to escape. Torn and bleeding, they broke free and scurried away, their tails curled under to ward off the nips from the chasing victors.

The three golden jackals only gave up the chase when they had forced the silver-backs to dive dangerously through the legs of a herd of wildebeeste, whereat triumphant, they returned to the kill.

Moshi watched while his two companions stretched out exhausted. They were young and the fur on their bodies was matted with burrs and mud. As they twitched in deep sleep he could see the white scars of the many bites they had suffered during the fight when their father had been killed by marauding jackals.

Moshi tried to groom the nearest jackal, but it whined in sleepy protest and he gave up. Resting his head on its shoulder, he listened as the distant cackles of a hyena pack broke the rhythmic cropping of the grazers. With the easy killing they had reverted to hunters and had left the scavenging to his kind.

As the sounds faded, the grazers resumed browsing and he relaxed and, enjoying the warmth from his companions' bodies, dozed.

*

Though the vast majority of the migrants were wildebeeste and zebra, amongst them mingled the smaller herds of eland, hartebeeste and topi. These, without the protective shield of the majority, very quickly became the target of hunting predators, eager for a change in diet.

Soon, the united jackals were aggressively defending the remains of these animals from the silver-backs, but this was not for long. As the grass was eaten down so the herds massed and again the urgency to find fresh grazing drove them on.

Once more the pickings became lean as the predators left little of their prey for scavengers.

The silver-backs dominated. Living naturally in the highlands, they out-hunted the golden jackals in the search for carrion in the woods and grasslands.

Sometimes, the three savanna jackals found the remains of an animal first, but before they had snatched a few bites the silver-backs would arrive in a pack to chase them from it.

Finally, when they had been beaten from a dead eland in a fight with six silver-backs, Moshi led the other two back to the migrating herds and a nomadic life. He loped through the shortened grass in angry silence. Hunger drove him and he didn't break his pace until they were amongst the trailing animals at the rear of the main herds.

Panting, the two jackals flopped down while Moshi sat watching the herds. After a few moments he stiffened as his sharp eyes caught a fleeting glimpse of possible prey darting in amongst the other animals.

With ears pricked up he trotted nearer to the migrators and crouching, stared into the forest of legs.

He remained frozen with a front paw hanging, forgotten in mid-stride. Then with a yap of triumph, he dived unheeding between the trooping animals.

They shied and snorted in protest but he was gone.

The relaxing jackals started to their feet at Moshi's yap and stood nervously looking for him.

Scared by his disappearance they raced around the zebra and wildebeeste barking for him. Then they stopped and pricked their ears up when they heard him yapping from the depths of the herds.

Suddenly, a Thomson gazelle buck bolted out with Moshi in pursuit. He jumped at it, missed and stumbling, fell on his side. The brothers streaked past him. Winded, Moshi limped after them.

The gazelle bounded on to the remains of a termite hill and warded off the attacking jackals with sharp stabs from its long horns. Harassed by the two, Moshi slunk round behind and leapt up, sinking his teeth into its tail.

With a squeal, the gazelle swung round dragging Moshi off balance, but with Moshi's full weight, the gazelles' backlegs folded and it skidded down the mound.

Fallen, the Thomson gazelle was at the jackals' mercy. They tore the helpless creature to death.

*

With the months of following the jackals learnt to anticipate the migrants movements. But one day, as they were moving beside the herds, a new restlessness overtook them. Large groups of wildebeeste broke away in a gallop, bellowing and kicking in defiance as they went. Gradually, the restlessness spread to the other animals, until thousands were thundering around in a frenzy.

The frightened jackals scurried for the safety of a kopje. Bewildered, they watched as the black mass of animals continued their erratic display, streaming past them to vanish from sight down a gorge.

At dawn the following day, the sounds faded and the jackals ventured down. The ground was pitted and scarred with millions of hoof prints and where there had once been green vegetation, dust devils were starting. They trotted along the trail of destruction and paused on the lip of the gorge.

Moshi barked with delight and skidded to the bottom. The hordes had followed a dried-up river bed and where they had torn back the overhanging trees and bushes in their rush, the vast expanse of the savannah was visible below, now green with freshly sprung grass.

Chapter Eight

On the plains the jackals trotted one behind the other through the damp grass, panting from the humid heat. Above them, gathering rain clouds rumbled ominously.

Moshi laid his ears flat at the sound and pausing sniffed into a gust of wind rustling the grass. Smelling rain, he put his front paws on one of his companions back and stood up on his hindlegs. He heard the excited barks of zebra, but the waving tips of the grass blew into his face and he blinked his eyes shut. When he opened them he snorted, startled by the sight of zebra and wildebeeste racing for a column of torrential rain heading towards him.

Whining to the others, he dropped down and ran back with them along the way they had come but it was too late. Heavy rain drops splattered into the grass and they huddled together as the downpour shrouded them in a grey mantle.

It hammered through their coats soaking them to the skin. Moshi stood, shook himself and scratched at the fleas, then shook himself again. Refreshed he watched the blurred shapes of the grass-eaters galloping with pleasure as the rain washed the dust and parasites from their bodies.

Infected by their friskiness, Moshi yapped, and dashed through a shallow depression full of muddy water, showering his companions.

Snorting, they cringed away, brushing at their muzzles. Then baiting them further, he rolled in the mud until he was thoroughly coated and standing over them, vigorously shook it off.

The mud-splattered jackals, growled, then gave chase. Soon, all three were romping through the wet grass like frolicking cubs, chasing their tails and sliding around in rough and tumble games, until the rain ceased and they took up the search of food once more.

Within weeks of the return of the migrants to the savannah, the wildebeeste and zebra and other game had spread and were grazing in small herds over the vast expanse. Moshi and his friends remained together and survived by hunting the abundance of small game. Eagerly, they raided the birds' nests for eggs and openly crossed other jackals' territory in pursuit of spring hares. When a predator made a kill the three of them were a match against paired jackals and would chase them away claiming it for themselves.

Once, while they were feeding off the meagre remains of a cheetah's kill, a herd of wildebeeste nearby stirred uneasily as a young male slowly walked towards the dominant bull tossing its head in challenge. Snorting, the bull faced the challenger and pawed at the ground, for a few moments the beasts stood silently eyeing each other then lowered their heads and charged.

At the crack of their clashing horns Moshi looked up, startled. Then seeing the cause of the sounds, dismissed the duelling wildebeeste with a grunt and returned to sniffing for abandoned scraps.

With locked horns the contestants grunted and strained. Suddenly, the young bull broke free and, twisting to the side, tried to escape. The old bull drove forward and his horns smacked into his adversary's haunches and before the stricken animal's bellows of pain had ceased, the jackals had raced into the foray.

Bewildered, the old bull sniffed at his antagonist then snorted in triumph and returned to his herd.

The young bull lay on its side groaning, blood was pouring from a deep gash in its underside and one back leg was broken.

The scent of blood deceived the jackals and they moved in to feed. Hearing them approach, the wildebeeste struggled up on to its front legs.

The two younger jackals stopped and stood nervously watching Moshi. He crouched down, staring at the wildebeeste straining to rise. It grunted and, just as it was standing on three legs, he dived under its stomach and tore at the wound.

Bellowing, the wildebeeste fought to remain upright. It stumbled, hopped, then regaining its balance unleashed two savage kicks to the side with its back leg. A hoof struck the nearest young jackal in the neck sending it spinning into the air. The other jackal yelped and fell as the second kick slammed into its ribs.

Still bellowing the enraged wildebeeste pivoted on its front legs and lashed out at Moshi. Cringing, he crawled into the safety of untrampled grass. The wildebeeste hobbled after him but jerked to a halt as its broken leg jarred against the ground. Shocked by the sudden pain, the wildebeeste lifted the broken leg above the grass and ran stumbling on three legs towards the herd.

Moshi crept back to his companions. Gently, he nuzzled one, then licked it and moaned softly. Its neck was broken and flies fed on the dark blotch of blood outlining the imprint of the hoof. The other jackal lifted its head. Yapping, Moshi leapt over the corpse and licked it all over its face. It wagged its tail feebly in response. The jackal raised himself unsteadily on its paws. Moshi wagged his tail and trotted ahead. His companion made a step to follow him then choked, spluttered and spat. Moshi ran back. Blood was trickling down its jaws. He licked it off and whining coaxed it to move again.

Frequently, the jackal stopped, stuggling to breathe but each time Moshi coaxed it on. When they reached the shade of a thorn bush the jackal wheezed and collapsed. Moshi yapped and playfully pressed his nose against its muzzle. The jackal did not move. As he backed away uncertain the jackal gave a cough and sighed. Moshi barked and wagging his tail ran into the grass returning a few minutes later with a half chewed rat. He whined softly, but the jackal remained silent. Dropping the rat between its paws he affectionately nuzzled the jackal, then his hackles bristling, he leapt back and let out a mournful howl.

*

Two golden jackals lay warming themselves in the early morning sun. Close by, a wildebeeste herd browsed peacefully. The jackals pricked their ears up as they heard the soft moans of a cow wildebeeste. They stood up and watched it, heavy with a calf, moving away from the herd, then followed. Ignoring the prowling jackals the cow stopped and began to give birth.

The muscles along the underside of her stomach contracted. Slowly the front legs of the calf appeared between her back legs. The cow glanced back, then she groaned and heaved. The calf slipped from her to the ground and burst out of its caul. The cow jumped, twisting in the air, and landed facing her calf on her front knees. She licked it.

The jackals crept forward, watching the calf as it tottered on its spindly legs trying to reach its mother's teats. The cow snorted and moved away. The calf staggered after her. Then the male jackal sprung forward and snatched up the afterbirth. Unconcerned the wildebeeste cow continued to evade the calf's attempts to feed until it could run.

When the jackals had finished, the male stood watching the wildebeeste, while his mate stretched out sunning herself. He tensed, excited by the sight of a wildebeeste hobbling on three legs and calling to his mate headed towards it. She shook herself and padded after him.

The mate paused and raised his leg marking a tuft of grass with his scent and trotted on. The female jackal just sniffed the tuft and followed.

All at once the male stopped, the hair on his back bristled as, growling, he approached the thorn bush where Moshi's dead companion lay.

Hidden in the grass, Moshi curled back his lip in a silent snarl and waited. Then, as the jackal bent his head to nose under the bush, he leapt on to him, sinking his teeth into the back of his neck.

The jackal yelped and struggled to free himself as Moshi growled and his teeth sank

deeper. The jackal whimpered and, at the same time, Moshi saw the female jackal. Startled he let go and backed away, but she made no move to attack him. Taking advantage of the respite, the male jackal flew at him. Moshi swerved to one side and bit deep into one of its legs, it let out a wail and fell on its back. Moshi sprang forward and savaged him in the stomach. Yelping the jackal rolled on to his feet and fled.

Moshi snarled at the female jackal and circled her. She lay crouched, her ears pressed back against her head. He moved closer. Her hackles bristled, but she let him smell her. He wagged his tail. She snarled at him and curled up, pretending to sleep. Indignant, Moshi stalked away, then stopped and looked back to catch her sneaking a glance at him. He turned away quickly, and lay down with his back to her.

The jackals continued to glance at each other when they thought that the other was not looking. At last Moshi crept towards her and lay down. She remained pretending to be asleep. Tentatively he licked her. She tensed slightly but did not move. Then lifting her head, the female jackal gently brushed her nose against his muzzle and licked him.

*

Moshi paused in his territorial hunt to mark his scent on a tuft of grass. His mate, trotted up behind him, and sniffed it and added her own.

They both pricked their ears up as they heard the familiar cackles of distant hyenas. The breeze ruffled Moshi's fur as he stood watching the vultures wheeling in the sky, plummetting to earth to feed. He whined softly to his mate, then moved towards them.

First published in Great Britain by
Rex Collings Ltd, 69 Marylebone High Street, London W1

© T. A. S. Gibson 1977

ISBN 0860360547

Typesetting by Malvern Typesetting Services Ltd
Printed in Great Britain by The Pitman Press, Bath